# Fisher-Price®

## FIRST GRADE LEARNING PAD

### Start with English

MODERN PUBLISHING
A Division of Unisystems, Inc.
New York, New York 10022
UPC Series #49425

# NOTE TO PARENTS

Dear Parents:

Helping your children master their world through early learning is as easy as the Fisher-Price® Workbooks!

As your child's first and most important teacher, you can encourage your child's love of learning by participating in learning activities at home. Working together on the activities in each of the Fisher-Price® First Grade Workbooks will help your child build confidence, learn to reason, and develop reading, writing, math, and language skills.

Help make your time together enjoyable and rewarding by following these suggestions:

- Choose a quiet time when you and your child are relaxed.
- Provide a selection of writing materials (pens, pencils, or crayons).
- Only work on a few pages at a time. Don't attempt to complete every page if your child becomes tired or loses interest.
- Praise your child's efforts.
- Discuss each page. Help your child relate the concepts in the books to everyday experiences.

This title, Start With English, teaches the following essential skills:

√     identifying common nouns for people, places, and things
√     using capital letters for proper nouns and to start sentences
√     understanding singular and plural pronouns
√     using singular, plural, past, and present tense verbs
√     identifying common adjectives
√     comparing adjectives with -er and -est
√     using sentences to express complete ideas
√     punctuating complete sentences correctly
√     understanding place words such as in, under, and behind
√     creating and understanding compound words

Collect the entire series of Fisher-Price First Grade Learning Pads:

- Start With Phonics    • Start With Math
- Start With English    • Start to Read and Write

Some words name a **person**, **place**, or **thing**.

Look at the pictures and read the words.
Write two naming words in each list.

boy

house

car

doctor

farm

bed

**people**

_____
- - - - - - - - - - - - -
_____
- - - - - - - - - - - - -
_____

**places**

_____
- - - - - - - - - - - - -
_____
- - - - - - - - - - - - -
_____

**things**

_____
- - - - - - - - - - - - -
_____
- - - - - - - - - - - - -
_____

**Skills**: Identifying common nouns; Writing

Some words name **people**.

clown

girl

Color each space that has a word
that names a person.
What do you see?

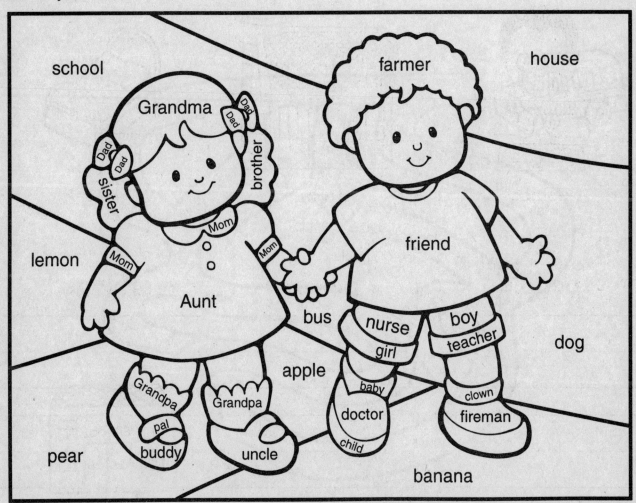

**Skills**: Identifying common nouns for people

Some words name **places**.

store

city

Help the bus get to the school.
Draw a line through the maze.
Follow the path with the words that name places.

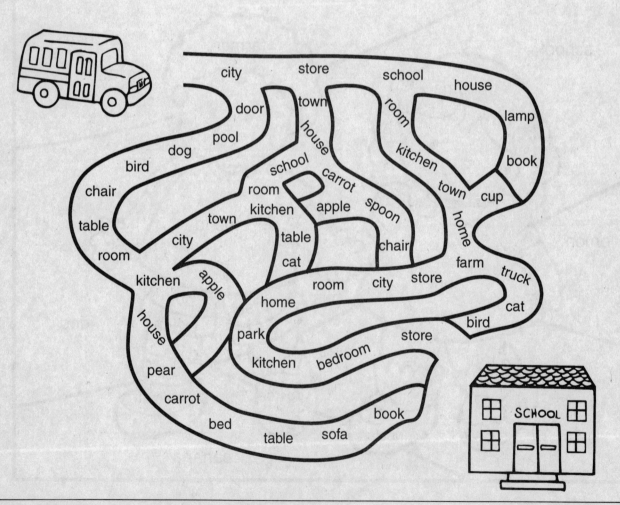

**Skills**: Identifying common nouns for places

Some words name **things**.

clock           ball

Find the words that name things in the puzzle.

table

truck

lamp

cup

moon

book

X T R U C K D
C A V M L R F
Y B O O K L Q
E L J O B A Y
K E T N M M J
H R S C U P C
P M L V F W G

---

**Skills**: Identifying common nouns for things

**People**, **places**, and **pets** have special names.
The special names begin with **capital letters**.
Write the special names in the sentences.

### Bob

The man's name is

_____

### Grandma

The woman is

_____

### Tippy

The cat's name is

_____

### Elm Street

They live on

_____

My name is _____

_____

**Skills**: Understanding proper nouns; Writing capital letters

The **days** of the week begin with **capital letters**.

Sonya Lee made a list of things to do this week.
Read her list.
Write the day of the week in each sentence.

| Sunday | Monday | Tuesday | Wednesday |
|---|---|---|---|
| Play with friends. | Sing a song. | Play ball. | Read a book. |

| Thursday | Friday | Saturday |
|---|---|---|
| Go to birthday party. | Visit Grandpa | Make a new list! |

1. Sonya Lee will go to a party on _____

2. Sonya Lee will sing a song on _____

3. Sonya Lee will visit Grandpa on _____

4. Sonya Lee will make a new list on _____

**Skills**: Learning days of the week; Writing words with capital letters

The **months** of the year begin with **capital letters**.
Trace the months of the year.

| fall | winter |
|------|--------|
| September | December |
| October | January |
| November | February |

| spring | summer |
|--------|--------|
| March | June |
| April | July |
| May | August |

My birthday is in _____.

**Skills**: Learning the months of the year; Writing words with capital letters

Have a swingin' good time with books!

**He**, **she**, and **it** are special **naming words**.
They can be used to name people in a different way.

# The girl dances.
# <u>She</u> dances.

Read the sentences.
Write **he**, **she**, or **it**.

## The boy has a hammer.

_____ has a hammer.

## The hot dog is on the plate.

_____ is on the plate.

## The girl rides the bike.

_____ rides the bike.

**Skills**: Using pronouns (he, she, and it)

**We** and **they** are also special naming words.

You and I can play ball.
<u>We</u> play ball.

Carlos and Sam wear glasses.
<u>They</u> wear glasses.

Read the sentences.
Write **we** or **they**.

You and I can build a sand castle.

_____ can build a sand castle.

The children know the alphabet.

_____ know the alphabet.

The boys are playing hockey.

_____ are playing hockey.

**Skills**: Using pronouns (we and they)

Always write I with a **capital letter**.

Write a capital I to complete each sentence.

Grandma and _____ went for a walk.

_____ held the dog's leash.

Grandma said _____ was a big help.

**Skills**: Using pronouns (I)

Some words show **action**.

**throw**

**catch**

Write the correct **action** word under each picture.

| paint | walk | slide | wave |

_____

_____

_____

_____

**Skills**: Identifying action words; Writing verbs

Add **s** to an **action** word to tell about **one person** or **thing**.

Two puppies bark.    One puppy barks.

Write the correct action word in each sentence.

wave

waves

The farmer _____ to her friend.

swim

swims

The pirates _____ to the shore.

walk

walks

Two children _____ down the path.

**Skills**: Adding -s to action words; Identifying subject-verb agreement

Add **ed** to an **action** word to tell about something that **already happened**.

Today the dogs bark.
Yesterday they barked.

Add **ed** to each word in the box.
Write the correct word in each sentence.
The first one is done for you.

| pick | walk | shop | ask |
|------|------|------|-----|

Yesterday I ___shopped___ with Mom.

We _____ to the store.

I _____ for some fruit.

I _____ red apples.

---

**Skills**: Adding -ed to action words; Identifying past and present tense

Read each sentence.
Add **s** or **ed** to a word in the box to finish each sentence.
Write the word in the puzzle.

| | | | |
|---|---|---|---|
| cook | play | smell | comb |

**Across**

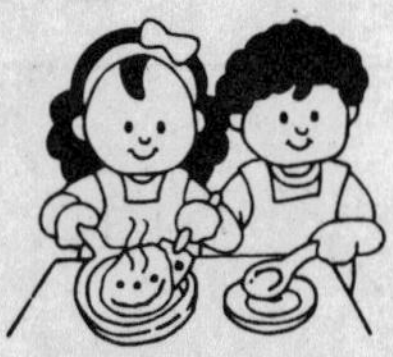

2. Yesterday we ______ dinner.

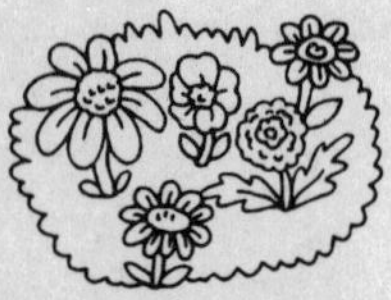

3. Today she ________ the flowers.

**Down**

1. Last night the children ______ .

2. Now she ________ her hair.

**Skills**: Adding -s or -ed to verbs

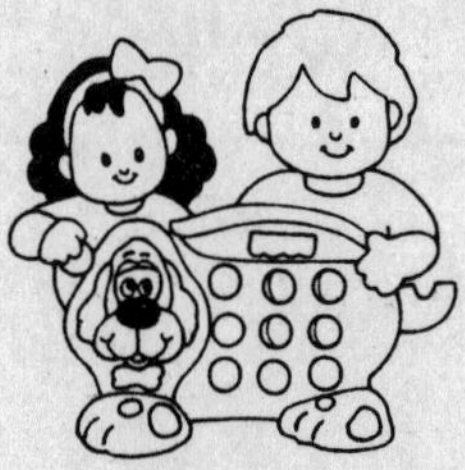

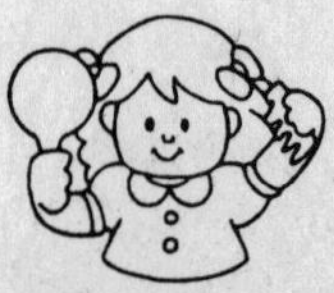

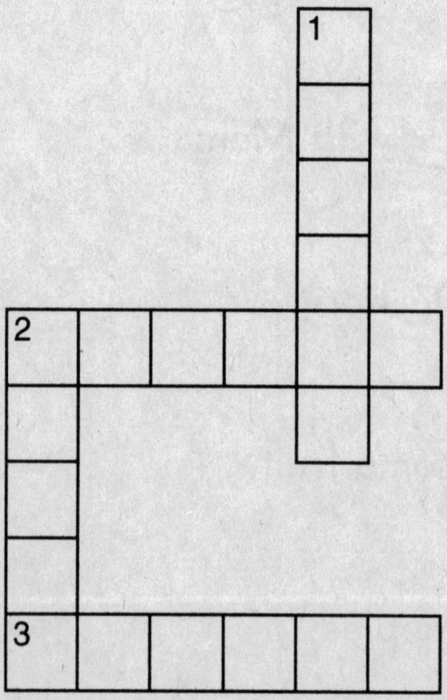

The **action** words **is** and **are** tell about what is **happening now**.

Use **is** to tell about **one person** or **thing**.
Use **are** to tell about **more than one**.

Circle **is** or **are** to complete each sentence.
Then finish coloring the picture.

| The boys | is are | playing. | The table legs | is are | straight. |
| The balls | is are | round. | One boy | is are | curly-haired. |
| The table | is are | a rectangle. | One ball | is are | near the pocket. |

**Skills**: Using is and are

The **action** words **was** and **were** tell about what happened in the **past**.

Use **was** to tell about **one person** or **thing**.
Use **were** to tell about **more than one**.

Write **was** or **were** to complete each sentence.

The man and woman _____ waving.

The dog _____ barking.

They all _____ walking.

**Skills**: Using was and were

Peek into the wonderful world of reading!

The action word **go** tells about what is happening **now**.
The action word **went** tells about what happened in the **past**.

Write **go** or **went** to complete each sentence.

Last week we _____ to see the eggs.

Today we _____ to see baby birds.

Last year I _____ to school by bus.

Now I _____ to school on foot.

**Skills**: Using go and went

The action word **see** tells about what is happening **now**.
The action word **saw** tells about what happened in the **past**.

Write **see** or **saw** to complete each sentence.

Last week I_____
a lion.

Now I_____
a clown.

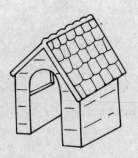

Yesterday I_____
a doghouse.

Today I_____
a dog.

**Skills**: Using see and saw

**Describing** words tell about a **person**, **place**, or **thing**.

Read the describing words in the box.
Write the correct describing word to complete each sentence.
The first one is done for you.

| loud | fast | strong | tall |
|------|------|--------|------|

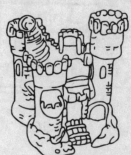

The castle has two ___tall___ towers.

The cannon made a _____ noise.

The knight has a _____ shield.

The knights ride _____ horses.

**Skills**: Identifying describing words; Writing adjectives

**Describing** words tell about **colors**.
Color the markers to match the labels.

Then read the color words and color the picture.

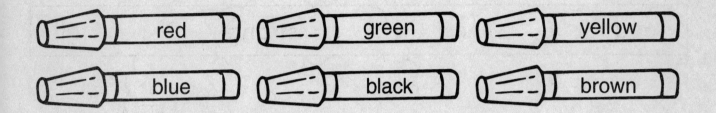

red    green    yellow

blue    black    brown

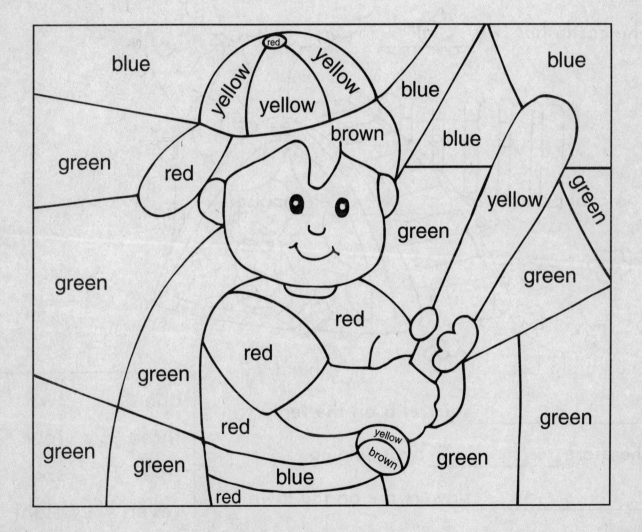

What color is the boy's shirt? _____

**Skills**: Recognizing color words

**Describing** words tell **how many**.
Write the word that tells how many to complete each sentence.

_____ squirrel is on the tent.

There are _____ birds singing.

_____ flowers are on the lawn.

There are _____ fenceposts.

| | |
|---|---|
| one | two |
| three | four |
| five | six |
| seven | eight |
| nine | ten |

**Skills**: Recognizing number words; Counting

**Describing** words tell about **size**.

Read each sentence.
**Circle** the word that tells the **size**.
Then draw a **line** from the word to the picture.

1. The ladder is tall.

2. Where is the small bear?

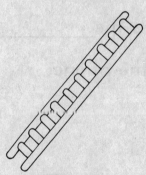

3. The tiny bird sits on the perch.

4. The little baby plays with the ball.

5. The girl on TV pats a large horse.

**Skills**: Recognizing words for size

**Describing** words tell about **shape**.

**round**   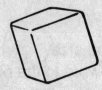 **square**

Write the describing word that tells the **shape** to complete each sentence.

Press the _____ buttons
on the phone.

The house has a _____
door.

The girl made _____
bubbles.

I can eat the _____
sandwich.

**Skills**: Recognizing words for shape

Add **er** to a **describing** word to show the difference between **people** or **things**.

**This boy is young.**   **This baby is younger.**

Look at the pictures.
Write the words.

small _____

tall _____

fast _____

**Skills**: Adding -er to compare two things

Add **est** to a **describing** word to show the difference between **people** or **things**.

**old**      **older**      **oldest**

Draw a line from the describing word to the picture.

long

longest

longer

tallest

taller

tall

**Skills**: Adding -est to compare more than two things

Learning the ABCs of mountain climbing!

**Describing** words tell how things **sound**.

Look at the pictures.
Describe the sounds by drawing a line to **loud** or **soft**.

**Skills**: Recognizing words for sounds

**Describing** words tell how things **feel**.

The words in the box tell how things feel.
Read the clues. Write the words in the puzzle.

| hot | cool | dry | wet | light | heavy |

**Across**

2. Snow feels _____.

5. A trunk feels _____.

6. Rain feels _____.

**Down**

1. The sun feels _____.

3. A pillow feels _____.

4. Sand feels _____.

**Skills**: Recognizing words that describe how things feel

**Describing** words tell how things **taste** or **smell**.

Trace the words that describe how things taste or smell.
Find the words in the puzzle.

| salty | sweet | tart | delicious | fresh | sour |

fresh

salty

sweet

sour

delicious

tart

```
e  l  i  n  b  e  j  l  f
b  s  a  l  t  y  r  s  r
o  w  r  e  s  c  k  o  e
d  e  l  i  c  i  o  u  s
i  e  k  o  g  s  t  r  h
b  t  a  r  t  e  i  v  z
```

**Skills**: Recognizing words that describe how things taste and smell

A telling sentence tells something.

It must tell a complete idea.
Draw a line under the complete telling sentences.
The first one is done for you.

have an apple

<u>I have an apple.</u>

The children slide.

The children

to rock.

The baby likes to rock.

We

We ride.

**Skills**: Identifying sentences

A sentence starts with a **capital letter**.
A telling sentence ends with a **period**.
Write each telling sentence correctly.
The first one is done for you.

the pumpkin is bright orange

The pumpkin is bright orange.

i have a heart on my dress

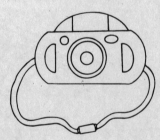

the camera can take pictures

**Skills**: Identifying declarative sentences; using a capital letter and a period

An asking sentence asks something.

Read each asking sentence.
Draw a line to match the question to the picture.

Where does the horse live?

How many wheels are on
the van?

Who is holding the kite?

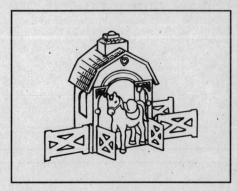

What is Grandpa carrying?

**Skills**: Identifying interrogative sentences

A sentence starts with a **capital letter**.
An asking sentence ends with a **question mark**.
Trace the question mark, then draw your own.

Write each asking sentence correctly.

who wears the pirate hat

_____

how many barrels are on the boat

_____

does a pirate wear a mask

_____

**Skills**: Identifying interrogative sentences; using a capital letter and a question mark

A good book and a good banana make great bedtime treats!

Some words tell where things are.

# The boy is **on** the horse.

The words in the box tell where things are.
Read the clues.
Write the words in the puzzle.

| under | in | out | at | behind | over |

**Across**   2. The dog is
_____
of the house.

4. The animals
are _____
the fence.

**Down**   1. The boy writes
_____
the table.

2. The plane flew
_____
the house.

3. The swing is
_____
the branch.

5. The pig is
_____
the mud.

**Skills**: Identifying words that tell where things are

**Compound** words are two words that are put together to make one word.

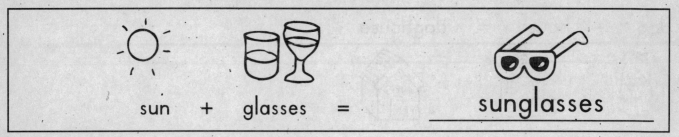

sun   +   glasses   =   _sunglasses_

Look at the pictures and read the words.
Write the **compound** words.
Then draw a picture to show the new compound word.

cup   +   cake   =   _____

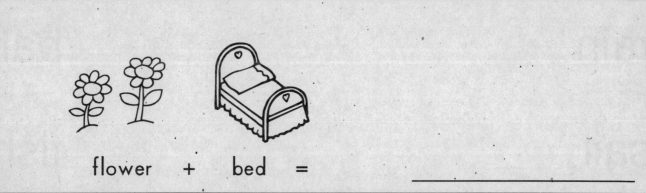

flower   +   bed   =   _____

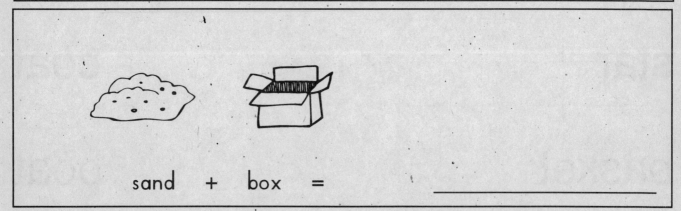

sand   +   box   =   _____

**Skills**: Identifying compound words

A **compound** word is made from two words.

dog + house = doghouse

Look at the pictures.
Draw a line to match the words.

  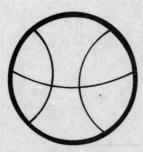 

rain                                    ball

sail                                    fish

star                                    coat

basket                                  boat

**Skills:** Identifying compound words

# ANSWER KEY

## Page 5

Some words name **people**.

clown  girl

Color each space that has a word that names a person. What do you see?

school · house
lemon
bus
apple · dog
pear
banana

## Page 6

Some words name **places**.

store · city

Help the bus get to the school.
Draw a line through the maze.
Follow the path with the words that name places.

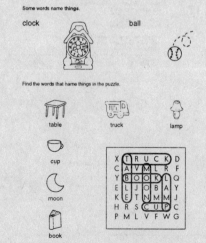

## Page 7

Some words name **things**.

clock · ball

Find the words that name things in the puzzle.

table · truck · lamp
cup
moon
book

| X | T | R | U | C | K | D |
| C | A | V | M | L | R | F |
| Y | E | B | O | O | K | Q |
| L | L | J | O | B | L | J |
| E | E | T | N | M | M | J |
| H | R | S | C | U | P | C |
| P | M | L | V | F | W | G |

## Page 8

**People**, **places**, and **pets** have special names.
The special names begin with **capital letters**.
Write the special names in the sentences.

Bob · Grandma

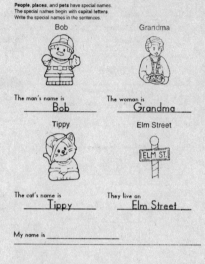

The man's name is ___Bob___

The woman is ___Grandma___

Tippy · Elm Street

The cat's name is ___Tippy___

They live on ___Elm Street___

My name is _____

## Page 9

The **days** of the week begin with **capital letters**.

Sonya Lee made a list of things to do this week.
Read her list.
Write the day of the week in each sentence.

| Sunday | Monday | Tuesday | Wednesday |
|---|---|---|---|
| Play with friend. | Sing a song. | Play ball. | Read a book. |

| Thursday | Friday | Saturday |
|---|---|---|
| Go to birthday party. | Visit Grandpa. | Make a new list! |

1. Sonya Lee will go to a party on ___Thursday___

2. Sonya Lee will sing a song on ___Monday___

3. Sonya Lee will visit Grandpa on ___Friday___

4. Sonya Lee will make a new list on ___Saturday___

## Page 10

The **months** of the year begin with **capital letters**.
Trace the months of the year.

| fall | winter |
|---|---|
| September | December |
| October | January |
| November | February |

| spring | summer |
|---|---|
| March | June |
| April | July |
| May | August |

My birthday is in _____

# ANSWER KEY

**Page 12**

He, she, and it are special **naming words**.
They can be used to name people in a different way.

The girl dances.
<u>She</u> dances.

Read the sentences.
Write he, she, or it.

The boy has a hammer.
<u>He</u> has a hammer.

The hot dog is on the plate.
<u>It</u> is on the plate.

The girl rides the bike.
<u>She</u> rides the bike.

**Page 13**

We and they are also special naming words.
You and I can play ball.
<u>We</u> play ball.

Carlos and Sam wear glasses.
<u>They</u> wear glasses.

Read the sentences.
Write we or they.

You and I can build a sand castle.
<u>We</u> can build a sand castle.

The children know the alphabet.
<u>They</u> know the alphabet.

The boys are playing hockey.
<u>They</u> are playing hockey.

**Page 14**

Always write I with a **capital letter**.

Write a capital I to complete each sentence.

Grandma and <u>I</u> went for a walk.

<u>I</u> held the dog's leash.

Grandma said <u>I</u> was a big help.

**Page 15**

Some words show action.

throw    **catch**

Write the correct action word under each picture.

| paint | walk | slide | wave |

<u>slide</u>    <u>paint</u>

<u>walk</u>    <u>wave</u>

**Page 16**

Add **s** to an **action** word to tell about **one person** or **thing**.

Two puppies bark.    One puppy barks.

Write the correct action word in each sentence.

wave
waves

The farmer <u>waves</u> to her friend.

swim
swims

The pirates <u>swim</u> to the shore.

walk
walks

Two children <u>walk</u> down the path.

**Page 17**

Add **ed** to an **action** word to tell about something that **already happened**.

Today the dogs bark.
Yesterday they barked.

Add **ed** to each word in the box.
Write the correct word in each sentence.
The first one is done for you.

| pick | walk | shop | ask |

Yesterday I <u>shopped</u> with Mom.

We <u>walked</u> to the store.

I <u>asked</u> for some fruit.

I <u>picked</u> red apples.

# ANSWER KEY

**Page 18**

Read each sentence.
Add **s** or **ed** to a word in the box to finish each sentence.
Write the word in the puzzle.

| cook | play | smell | comb |

**Across**                                      **Down**

2. Yesterday we <u>cooked</u> dinner.     1. Last night the children <u>played</u> .

3. Today she <u>smells</u> the           2. Now she <u>combs</u> her hair.
flowers.

```
        p
        l
        a
        y
c o o k e d
o       d
m
b
s m e l l s
```

**Page 19**

The **action** words **is** and **are** tell about what is **happening now.**

Use **is** to tell about **one person** or **thing.**
Use **are** to tell about **more than one.**

Circle **is** or **are** to complete each sentence.
Then finish coloring the picture.

| The boys | (is)/are | playing. | The table legs | is/(are) | straight. |
| The balls | is/(are) | round. | One boy | (is)/are | curly-haired. |
| The table | (is)/are | a rectangle. | One ball | (is)/are | near the pocket. |

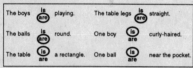

**Page 20**

The **action** words **was** and **were** tell about what happened in the **past.**

Use **was** to tell about **one person** or **thing.**
Use **were** to tell about **more than one.**

Write **was** or **were** to complete each sentence.

The man and woman <u>were</u> waving.

The dog <u>was</u> barking.

They all <u>were</u> walking.

**Page 22**

The action word **go** tells about what is happening **now.**
The action word **went** tells about what happened in the **past.**

Write **go** or **went** to complete each sentence.

Last week we <u>went</u> to        Today we <u>go</u> to
see the eggs.                      see baby birds.

Last year I <u>went</u> to        Now I <u>go</u> to school
school by bus.                    on foot.

**Page 23**

The action word **see** tells about what is happening **now.**
The action word **saw** tells about what happened in the **past.**

Write **see** or **saw** to complete each sentence.

Last week I <u>saw</u>            Now I <u>see</u>
a lion.                           a clown.

Yesterday I <u>saw</u>           Today I <u>see</u>
a doghouse.                       a dog.

**Page 24**

**Describing** words tell about a **person, place,** or **thing.**

Read the describing words in the box.
Write the correct describing word to complete each sentence.
The first one is done for you.

| loud | fast | strong | tall |

The castle has two <u>tall</u> towers.

The cannon made a <u>loud</u> noise.

The knight has a <u>strong</u> shield.

The knights ride <u>fast</u> horses.

# ANSWER KEY

**Page 25**

Describing words tell about **colors**.
Color the markers to match the labels.

Then read the color words and color the picture.

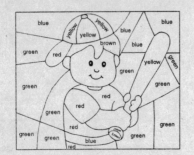

What color is the boy's shirt? ____red____

**Page 26**

Describing words tell how many.
Write the word that tells how many to complete each sentence.

____One____ squirrel is on the tent.

There are ____two____ birds singing.

____Five____ flowers are on the lawn.

There are ____seven____ fenceposts.

| | |
|---|---|
| one | two |
| three | four |
| five | six |
| seven | eight |
| nine | ten |

**Page 27**

Describing words tell about **size**.

Read each sentence.
Circle the word that tells the **size**.
Then draw a line from the word to the picture.

1. The ladder is (tall)

2. Where is the (small) bear?

3. The (tiny) bird sits on the perch.

4. The (little) baby plays with the ball.

5. The girl on TV pats a (large) horse.

**Page 28**

Describing words tell about **shape**.

round   **square**

Write the describing word that tells the **shape** to complete each sentence.

Press the ____round____ buttons on the phone.

The house has a ____square____ door.

The girl made ____round____ bubbles.

I can eat the ____square____ sandwich.

**Page 29**

Add **er** to a **describing** word to show the difference between **people** or **things**.

**This boy is young.**   **This baby is younger.**

Look at the pictures.
Write the words.

small        smaller

tall         taller

fast         faster

**Page 30**

Add **est** to a **describing** word to show the difference between **people** or **things**.

old        older        oldest

Draw a line from the describing word to the picture.

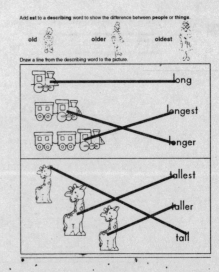

long

longest

longer

tallest

taller

tall

# ANSWER KEY

**Page 32**

Describing words tell how things **sound**.

Look at the pictures.
Describe the sounds by drawing a line to **loud** or **soft**.

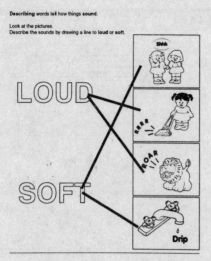

**Page 33**

Describing words tell how things **feel**.

The words in the box tell how things feel.
Read the clues. Write the words in the puzzle.

| hot | cool | dry | wet | light | heavy |
|-----|------|-----|-----|-------|-------|

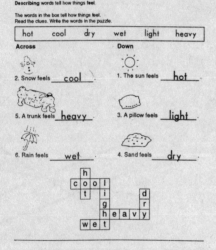

**Across**

2. Snow feels _cool_.

5. A trunk feels _heavy_.

6. Rain feels _wet_.

**Down**

1. The sun feels _hot_.

3. A pillow feels _light_.

4. Sand feels _dry_.

**Page 34**

Describing words tell how things **taste** or **smell**.

Trace the words that describe how things taste or smell.
Find the words in the puzzle.

| salty | sweet | tart | delicious | fresh | sour |
|-------|-------|------|-----------|-------|------|

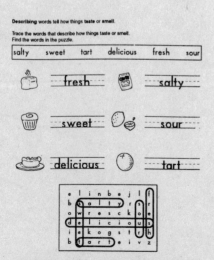

**Page 35**

A telling sentence tells something.

It must tell a complete idea.
Draw a line under the complete telling sentences.
The first one is done for you.

**Page 36**

A sentence starts with a capital letter.
A telling sentence ends with a period.
Write each telling sentence correctly.
The first one is done for you.

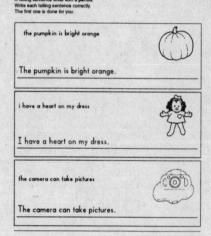

**Page 37**

An asking sentence asks something.

Read each asking sentence.
Draw a line to match the question to the picture.

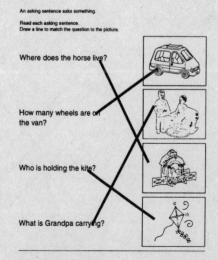

# ANSWER KEY

**Page 38**

A sentence starts with a **capital letter**.
An asking sentence ends with a **question mark**.
Trace the question mark, then draw your own.

Write each asking sentence correctly.

who wears the pirate hat

Who wears the pirate hat?

how many barrels are on the boat

How many barrels are on the boat?

does a pirate wear a mask

Does a pirate wear a mask?

**Page 40**

Some words tell where things are.

Thé boy is **on** the horse.

The words in the box tell where things are.
Read the clues.
Write the words in the puzzle.

under    in    out    at    behind    over

**Across**  2. The dog is _____ of the house.
4. The animals are _____ the fence.

**Down**  1. The boy writes _____ the table.
2. The plane flew _____ the house.
3. The swing is _____ the branch.
5. The pig is _____ the mud.

**Page 41**

Compound words are two words that are put together to make one word.

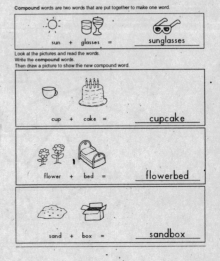

sun + glasses = sunglasses

Look at the pictures and read the words.
Write the **compound words**.
Then draw a picture to show the new compound word.

cup + cake = cupcake

flower + bed = flowerbed

sand + box = sandbox

**Page 42**

A **compound** word is made from two words.

dog + house = doghouse

Look at the pictures.
Draw a line to match the words.

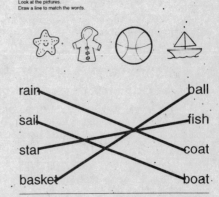

rain ————— ball
sail ————— fish
star ————— coat
basket ————— boat